# ANCIENT
## MAYA TRADERS
### OF AMBERGRIS CAYE

CAE

CARIBBEAN ARCHAEOLOGY AND ETHNOHISTORY
L. Antonio Curet, Series Editor

# ANCIENT
## MAYA TRADERS
## OF AMBERGRIS CAYE

Thomas H. Guderjan

With a New Preface by the Author

The University of Alabama Press
*Tuscaloosa*

Originally published by Cubola Productions, Belize, Central America; reprinted by the University of Alabama Press 2007 with additional photographs, new preface, and revised "Other Publications" section.

∞
The paper on which this book is printed meets the minimum requirements of American National Standard for Information Science—Permanence of Paper for Printed Library Materials, ANSI Z39.48-1984.

Ancient Maya traders of Ambergris Caye
Guderjan, Thomas H.

(Caribbean archaeology and ethnohistory)
("Fire Ant books")

ISBN-13 978-0-8173-5463-3 (pbk. : alk. paper)
ISBN-10 0-8173-5463-8 (pbk. : alk. paper)

                            •

Library of Congress Cataloging-in-Publication Data

Guderjan, Thomas H.
  Ancient Maya traders of Ambergris Caye / Thomas H. Guderjan with a new preface by the author.
      p. cm. —  (Caribbean archaeology and ethnohistory)
          "Fire Ant books."
  Originally published: Benque Viejo del Carmen, Belize : Cubola Productions, 1993.
  ISBN-13: 978-0-8173-5463-3 (pbk. : alk. paper)
  ISBN-10: 0-8173-5463-8
  1. Mayas—Commerce. 2. Mayas—Antiquities. 3. Ambergris Cay (Belize)—Antiquities.  I.
Title.
  F1435.3.C6G83 2007
  972.82′2—dc22
                            2007017367

Line drawings by Louise Bélanger first published in the *Journal of Field Anthropology,* vol. 16 (1989), in an article by Elizabeth Graham and David Pendergast. Line drawing on p. 39 by David M. Copher.

# Contents

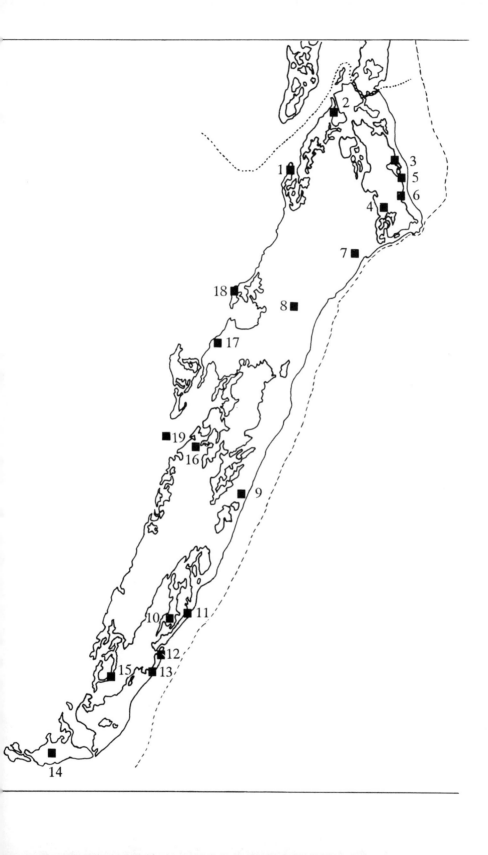

# ANCIENT
## MAYA TRADERS
### OF AMBERGRIS CAYE

# Preface

When this volume was originally published in Belize, the intent was to return something to the people of San Pedro who helped us over the course of three summers of fieldwork (1986–88). At that time, though we did not really know it yet, the town of San Pedro was just developing its tourism business. In 1986, we rented an entire hotel for $10 per day per room! And, I have a photo of First Street in mid-day with only a sleeping dog on the sand street. Today, both the dog and photographer would be run over by golf carts, taxis, or delivery vehicles within seconds.

Our work on Ambergris Caye was aimed at better understanding the ancient trade system that linked the great Maya kingdoms of the mainland. At the time, this was a hot topic among Maya archaeologists, and a half dozen other projects were ongoing along the Caribbean coast of Belize and Mexico—making the interaction among the researchers one of the most satisfying experiences of professional life. Of course, living in a tent camp on a Caribbean beach was not unpleasant either!

My co-directors of the project were Jim Garber and David Glassman of Southwest Texas State

University (now Texas State University) and Herman Smith of the Corpus Christi Museum in Texas. Each of us brought distinctive talents to the project, and without any one of us, it would not have been a success. Consequently, I received my doctoral degree, Jim and Dave were awarded tenure, and Herman soon retired to live in San Pedro for a number of years.

Our success was also a testament to the students from the SWT Archaeological Field School and the volunteers from the Corpus Christi Museum who worked so hard to support us. The Corpus Christi program eventually became the model and seed for the organization that I now direct. I recall that after the first week of fieldwork in the second season, we were camped about thirty miles from the town of San Pedro. We had no chairs and were almost out of water, gasoline, and food. The outboard motor on our boat had broken, and we could not make the two-way radio work despite our best efforts. We took the boat to the Mexican town of Xkalac where there should have been gasoline and water. However, when we arrived, they only had enough gas in town to get us back to our camp and our fifteen volunteers. Happily, there was no lack of cold beer in Xkalac, which served to improve camp attitudes hugely.

Eventually the cost of operating in San Pedro inspired Jim and I to found new projects in the Belize Valley and northwestern Belize, respectively, and our work on Ambergris closed after the 1988 season. Nevertheless, much remains to be done. I think of the doctoral dissertation level materials waiting for someone who wants to clarify the ceramic chronology or to look at the Postclassic materials at Laguna Francesa for example. Ambergris is developing rapidly, and someone should do this soon while the opportunity still exists.

Finally, I thank my co-directors of the project as well as all of the students and volunteers who made it possible. I especially thank Judith Knight of the University of Alabama Press for suggesting (or did she insist?) that this book should be republished.

Fort Worth, Texas
November 14, 2006

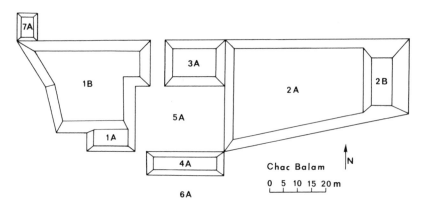

Planview of Chac Balam.

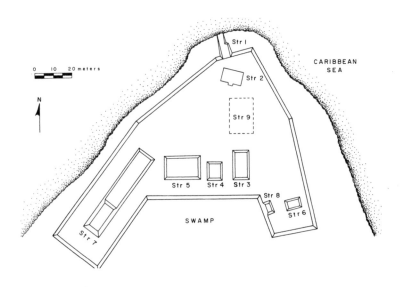

Planview of San Juan.

Traveling through the Boca Bacalar Chico, the cut that separates
Ambergris Caye, Belize, from mainland Mexico. The author
believes the cut was dug by the ancient Maya.

Tohil Plumbate vessel from San Juan. A nearly identical vessel
was found at Marco Gonzalez at the south end of Ambergris
Caye by the Royal Ontario Museum excavators. Tohil Plumbate was only made on the northwest coast of Guatemala.

A large Sotuta-style plate from a leader's burial at Chac
Balam. This and others were imported from the area of
Chichen Itza in the northern Yucatan Peninsula.

Punta San Juan on the northwest of Ambergris Caye. The
underwater line extending north is a recent feature. Punta
San Juan is the first landmark found after boating westward
through the Boca Bacalar Chico.

# The Maya

No one is sure when the first Maya came to Ambergris Caye. For that matter we do not even know when the first people became ethnically 'Maya'. However, there are many things which we do know about the ancient Maya civilization. Most importantly, this was a real civilization in every sense of the word. The Classic Maya had extremely complex political organizations, astronomers, engineers, and even a form of writing. Some Maya cities such as Tikal probably had over 100,000 people. Estimates of the population of the Classic Maya period are as large as three to five million people in the southern lowlands, which includes Belize and the Petén district of Guatemala. Within this civilization, now gone for a millennium, Ambergris Caye played an important role.

The rulers of the Maya civilization were much like kings. Each city-state was controlled by an individual who may have inherited his office because of his ancestry. Today we know that much of the writings and art of the Maya on their monuments and murals are records of the history of the ruling lineages. Monuments, or stelae, record much of this history. The importance of a ruler's lineage is reflected in the fact that his relationships to past rulers and their accomplishments are described in such detail on these monuments.

Maya astronomers were more astrologers than scientists. Our own astronomers ruminate about ideas such as the origins of the universe and how the various celestial bodies are related to each other. Maya astronomers, on the other hand, were much more interested in the effects events in the night sky had upon their lives and especially the lives of their rulers. The great achievements of the Maya were made by detailed observations of generations of skywatchers without the advantages of modern technology. They observed the sky for thousands of years and with such precision that their measurements of celestial events, such as the synodic period of Venus and the Maya calendar, were more precise than ours. The application of astronomic principles can be seen in some of their great architecture. At Chichén Itzá, they built a great observatory and designed the great pyramid, now called El Castillo, with 365 steps; one for each day of a year. El Castillo was designed with an orientation marking the vernal equinox as well. In Belize, Plaza B at Chan Chich and the main plaza at the site of Caracol may have been laid out to celebrate the summer and winter solstices.

For most people, the most startling and grand evidence we have today of the Maya civilization are their 'pyramids'. Unlike the Egyptian pyramids which were primarily tombs for the rulers, Maya pyramids were really simply huge substructural platforms. On the summit was usually a set of small rooms used by the religious elite. Occasionally, a ruler or another elite member of society was entombed in one of these buildings. However, their primary purpose was not for burial of the dead but for use by the living.

Archaeologists once thought of the Maya as having 'Old' and 'New' Empires with the 'Old Empire' based at the great center of Tikal and the 'New Empire' at Chichén Itzá. Today, we see the Maya civilization not as an empire controlled from a single city, but as a series of city-states. Despite decades of research, we are still unsure of the relationships among these large centers. Certainly they cooperated and competed with each other at different times. In the year 562 A.D., Lord Water, the ruler of Caracol, perhaps the largest ruin in Belize, conquered Tikal. For about 140 years, Tikal was dominated by Caracol. On the other hand, in 450 A.D. Stormy Sky, one of the greatest rulers of Tikal, may have installed his son, Six Sky, as the ruler of the city of Río Azul. While it is clear that each city-state controlled the surrounding region, we do not yet understand the nature of that control. Were smaller ceremonial centers vassals of the kings or were they largely independent? Though more research answers old questions, it often raises new ones which cannot be solved for years. The relationships between large and small Maya sites is one of those questions.

It is generally believed that Ambergris Caye was part of the city-state of Chetumal. Though the name of the Mexican port on Chetumal Bay was changed from Payo Obispo to Chetumal, ancient Chetumal was almost certainly at the site of Santa Rita on the outskirts of Corozal Town. Excavations at Santa Rita have shown that the kingdom

thrived into the 13th century, well after the general collapse of the Maya civilization. Here, again, the relationships among ancient communities become quite foggy. Were the smaller communities on Ambergris Caye closely integrated with Santa Rita or under Santa Rita's protection or were they independent from the mainland kingship?

Whatever the nature of the Maya political organization, trade and commerce are parts of the glue that holds all societies together. One of the major functions of all governments is to regulate the flow of goods among trading partners to the benefit of the state. Some archaeologists have thought that the origins of civilization itself may be perceived in the need for institutionalized trade and commerce. Once trade reaches the point where it is no longer simply casual exchange, institutions, sometimes private and sometimes public, must be established to cope with the flow of goods and resources. Certainly, the Maya were no exception to this.

It only takes a few minutes with a map of the Maya lowlands to understand the importance of coastal and riverine canoe trade. The rivers furthest north in Central America drain the Petén region of Guatemala into the Gulf of México and the Caribbean Sea. On the Caribbean side, the Río Hondo, the New River and their tributaries empty into Chetumal and Corozal Bays just behind Ambergris Caye. Ambergris acts as a barrier island to protect these bays.

The island also is a logical place for goods from the mainland to be brought and placed on board coastal trade canoes. In 1502, Columbus had encountered one of these canoes near the Bay Islands of Honduras. It was "an Indian canoe, as long as a galley and eight foot in breadth, laden with western commodities, which it likely belonged to the province of Yucatán" and had 25 people on board. In 1988 a French-Mexican team replicated the trip of such a canoe. In a single day, they canoed from the village of Xcalac, six miles north of Ambergris Caye, through the Bacalar Chico channel which separates Ambergris from the state of Quintana Roo, México, and then south to the San Pedro lagoon. The canoe covered nearly 30 miles in a single day's travel. The 16 foot replica canoe could hold about a ton of goods and was powered by six paddlers. Boats of the size met by Columbus could have carried four to five times as much cargo.

The canoe team's success with a square-rigged sail is interesting as well. Archaeologists have debated whether the Maya used sails on their canoes. While some murals appear to show sails, not all authorities agree. Having found that attaching a sail was so easy and useful, the French-Mexican team could not believe that the creators of huge cities, astronomy and calendrics would not have done the same.

Ambergris Caye's strategic location allowed mainland goods to be trans-shipped to the coastal trade routes and vice versa. Mainland northern Belize was known to have produced important agricultural products such as corn and cacao. Cacao was used by the Maya as a medium of exchange, a sort of money. It was consumed as both a beverage and mole, a sauce used for ritual occasions. Indeed, today's chocolate is little more than cacao and sugar.

In exchange, the mainland imported elite goods such as pottery, jade, obsidian and grinding stones made of volcanic basalt. Such goods were imports which aggrandized the elites. When such goods were not available in sufficient quantities, local counterparts or imitations were occasionally used. In North American society, Gucci bags and European luxury cars function in much the same manner. The Maya preferred basalt grinding stones over the local limestone as they did not fragment so easily. Indeed, it is simple to determine whether an ancient Maya ate corn ground by limestone or basalt. The limestone ground corn wore the people's teeth so badly that often just looking at the results is a painful experience. Other items, such as exotic pottery and jade, did not function better than their local counterparts. Instead, their owners were using them to mark their status. Not everyone today can afford diamond jewelry and, by the same token, not everyone in the past could afford jade ritual objects.

Other materials were also important as commodities rather than elite goods. For example, people who eat enough meat do not normally need to add salt to their diet. However, with the high populations of the mainland, it could not have been possible to supply adequate meat to everyone. Therefore, much salt was imported from the large salinas of northern Yucatán. Salt, then, was a commodity needed by everyone. Anyone who has experienced a salt deficiency in the tropics understands this very clearly. On northern Ambergris Caye, too, the lagoons provided salt until only a few decades ago. Although there was not enough to provide for the needs of the mainlanders, sea salt added an important facet to the economy of ancient Ambergris Caye.

Documents found recently in Seville indicate that during the 17th century, at least some Spaniards recognized the economic importance of the Ambergris salt sources. In 1565, the governor of Yucatán was petitioned for a concession to commercially harvest salt from lagoons near the Bay of Chetumal. It is not clear that the document refers to Ambergris Caye, but it is very likely. Nor do we know if the petitioner was successful.

Archaeologists deal with the chronology of the Maya civilization by dividing it into the Preclassic, Classic and Postclassic periods. These are further divided into smaller periods such as the 'Early Classic'. During the Preclassic, we see the development of the institutions, architecture and kingdoms which are more apparent later in the Classic period (300-900 A.D.). Across Corozal Bay from Ambergris Caye, is the site of Cerros near the mouth of the New River. During the Late Preclassic period (300 B.C.-300 A.D.) at Cerros, archaeologists have found evidence of large scale construction of public architecture. By about 300 B.C., the Maya transformed Cerros from a small coastal village into a large center for commerce and regional authority. In a single enormous phase of construction, they built a huge, 10-foot tall, platform and on top of that, a series of pyramids. The largest of these rises 90 feet above the top of the platform. By this time, Cerros had become a city encircled by a canal that drained water from the lowlying community and brought water to the fields surrounding the city. Cerros seems to have specialized in the control of trade in elite goods.

Unfortunately, it is nearly impossible to recover direct evidence of trade in salt, cacao or corn because these goods do not preserve as well as jade or basalt. To complicate the situation further, ancient people had a tendency to eat the evidence.

At Cerros, Structure 5 is a small building in the core zone of the site with stucco images of the city's rulers on its facade. Such facades have now been found at other sites including Lamanai and, perhaps La Milpa in Belize, Kinal and Uaxactún in Guatemala and Kohunlich in México, just north of the Belize border. That Cerros participated in this region-wide celebration of the leaders of cities during the Late Preclassic indicates that the site did, indeed, hold an important place in the Maya world. While such cities dominated the Late Preclassic landscape, many much smaller communities also existed; ranging from small rural residences to more elite groups with formal courtyard residences. How these smaller communities were integrated with the great towns and cities we do not yet know. Surely, though, the kingdoms of the Classic period had their roots well established in the Late Preclassic.

It has been found that by the Early Classic period (300 A.D.-600 A.D.), the architectural, political, commercial and social patterns of the fluorescence of Maya civilization had become institutionalized in Maya cities throughout Belize and northern Guatemala. This period usually is considered to begin in 292 A.D. when the Maya first erected a carved monument, or stela, at Tikal. Stelae were used to announce and mark major events and the sometimes exaggerated accomplishments of the rulers.

However, it was during the Late Classic period (600-900 A.D.), that the architectural grandeur reached its height at Belizean cities such as Altun Ha, Caracol, La Milpa, Lamanai, Lubaantun, and Xunantunich. It was also during the Late Classic that the Maya expanded their political hierarchies. Rulers of even relatively small Late Classic sites in the northwestern interior of Belize began to erect stelae. Populations had grown to such an extent that virtually none of the tropical rainforest could have remained. Erosion from hill slopes had begun to fill the canals that drained the agricultural fields of the bajos, or low-lying areas. Aside from the problems of coping with the needs of large populations, the Maya experienced intrusions by neighboring groups. While the elite rulers created a market for exotic goods and commodities such as salt became more and more necessary, they may have also created a separate merchant class over which they did not have authority. The picture of the Maya near the end of their civilization is one of a society under stress from many directions. The Classic Maya civilization 'collapsed' about 900 years after Christ. In the heartland of the southern lowlands, major construction ended, monuments were no longer built, populations declined and dispersed. However, not every city participated in the 'collapse'. Some, like Lamanai, saw continued construction of large buildings for another century. Others, like Santa Rita at the site of today's Corozal Town, saw the continuation of ruling lineages for several centuries more. In general, though, cities were abandoned, ending the political and commercial success of the Classic period. Those that survived may have done so because their strategic locations enabled them to continue participating in the re-ordering of society. Ambergris Caye also played a very important role during this Terminal Classic period.

The final period, known as the Postclassic, dates from about 1000 A.D. until the arrival of the Spanish. There were several attempts at revitalizing the Maya civilization during this time, particularly at Chichén Itzá, Mayapán and Tiho, now Mérida, in Yucatán, México. The Postclassic Maya, possibly under the commercial control of the Putún Maya from Veracruz who operated from Chichén Itzá, built a series of coastal ports, such as Isla Cerritos on the north coast of Yucatán, Tulum on the Caribbean coast and Ixpaatún on the north side of Chetumal Bay. Tulum and Ixpaatún were built on bluffs and defended against land assault by walls around their core zones. The island of Cozumel functioned as both port and home of shrines for the goddess Ixchel to which the Maya made pilgrimages.

# Ambergris Caye

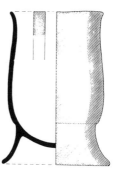

S ince the mid-1980s, two groups have been investigating the archaeology of Ambergris Caye. Elizabeth Graham and David Pendergast of the Royal Ontario Museum have worked at the site of Marco Gonzalez on the southern end of the island. The Ambergris Caye Archaeological Project, directed by Tom Guderjan of the University of Texas Institute of Texan Cultures at San Antonio, James Garber and David Glassman of Southwest Texas State University, and Herman Smith of the Corpus Christi Museum, spent four years finding and excavating ruins on the northern end. Together, we have been able to learn much of the Maya past at Ambergris.

When the Ambergris Caye Project started, our interest was in learning about the maritime trade of the Maya which must have occurred on Ambergris. We knew that coastal canoe trade had been a primary means of moving goods from one place to another in the Maya world. During the Postclassic period, it was thought that this trade had reached its zenith, but we knew relatively little about the mechanics of maritime trade before that time.

Ambergris Caye presented both opportunities and impediments to this sort of commerce. While Maya canoes could easily ply the waters between the coast and the reef, they would need to travel outside of the reef at Rocky Point on Ambergris Caye. At Rocky Point, the reef converges with the island, creating a beautiful and dramatic place but also one that is treacherous for boats even today. The Maya solved this problem by digging a channel across the peninsula at its narrowest point north of Rocky Point. Actually, Ambergris Caye is not an island but a part of México's Xcalac Peninsula, separated from the rest of the land and the country of México by an ancient canal. The Bacalar Chico canal was dug by 600 A.D., if not before. It was easier to dig a one mile long canal than it was to risk the loss of trade goods on the reef. Moreover, if the Maya could dig the much larger canal at Cerros by 300 B.C., certainly they could have dug the Bacalar Chico 900 years later.

The channel which separated Ambergris from México, then, was a 'funnel' for trade canoes. These canoes carried everything from salt and food to jade, obsidian, and pottery along the Caribbean coast. Columbus even encountered one which may have been 50 feet long and carried 25 people. Since Ambergris protects Chetumal and Corozal Bays from the open sea, the cut on the northern end, the Bacalar Chico, must have been an important access for the maritime traders. We also knew that the small site of San Juan was on the back side of the island and would be the first place a canoe would encounter after passing through the Bacalar Chico canal.

Based upon the excavations and surveys of Ambergris since 1985, we can now reconstruct the archaeology of the island to a large degree. The first known occupation of the island was at Marco Gonzalez where Graham and Pendergast have found deeply buried pottery fragments from the Late Preclassic period. Unfortunately, we know little of these early people except that they were there. Perhaps, these early artifacts are the remains of a fishing station or outpost from a larger mainland community such as Cerros.

Much the same is true of the Early Classic period which yields evidence of occupation at other sites, Laguna Francés and Yalamha, on the island. Laguna Francés is a large site by island standards and dates mostly to the Late Classic. However, some Early Classic pottery has been found in the back-dirt of areas disturbed by looters.

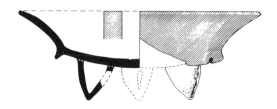

# Yalamha

Yalamha, literally 'under the water', is entirely submerged in about two feet of water near the entrance to Laguna Francés. Only a scatter of Early Classic pottery and stone artifacts, covering about 300 square meters, can now be found. This small residence may be a clue to why we cannot readily find Early Classic materials on Ambergris. We already know that relative sea level has risen about 50 centimeters since 100 A.D. and one meter since 1 A.D.. Not only have world-wide sea levels risen, but the geologic plate of which Ambergris and northern Belize are parts is tilting downward. Residents of the town of Corozal complain about the loss of their front yards to the bay during their lifetimes and the site of Cerros was once on the New River. With the expansion of the bay, Cerros is now several miles from the river's mouth. Likewise, Yalamha has sunk. As it did, wave action eroded away all of the soil and left the potsherds and stone tools to gradually drop onto the bedrock below the place where they had been used 1,300 or more years ago. If Yalamha, a very small residence on the edge of the coast, is representative of the Early Classic pattern, then it is unlikely that many other sites from this period will be found. In some cases such as at Laguna Francés, larger buildings were placed on top of the Early Classic remains and protected them from erosion.

By the Late Classic period, the coastal margins of the island had become heavily settled. San Juan, Chac Balam, Ek Luum, Punta Limón, Santa Cruz, Laguna Francés, San Pedro Lagoon, Tres Cocos, Habaneros, Burning Water, the Hancock site and Marco Gonzalez were occupied. It is during the Late Classic period that we see evidence of the greatest coastal population and the greatest diversity of sites.

A number of sites on the west side of Ambergris, Laguna Francés, San Juan and Chac Balam among them, share a number of features. Each of them have formal arrangements of small mounds which supported pole and thatch buildings and small plazas between the mounds. Each of them also either have good natural harbors or artificial harbors. We have also found relatively large amounts of exotic pottery, obsidian, basalt and ornamental greenstone. All of these things reflect the long distance trade which created wealth on the island. Like traders everywhere, from antique dealers to drug dealers, these ancient traders skimmed some of the cream off the top. So, the communities involved with trade were able to enjoy the 'Waterford crystal' of the day, so to speak. They also emulated the architecture of the mainland. This was both a reflection of their affluence and their need for formal and appropriate space in which to conduct business. The small plazas among their buildings were, in effect, offices and markets, where they could undertake their business. And, of course, coastal trade could not be serviced without a place to harbor boats. Indeed, most of these sites are located where natural harbors exist. Although, at Chac Balam, the Maya had to dig a harbor over 100 meters long so that boats could be secured.

# San Juan

San Juan juts into the water of the back side of Ambergris, just where boats could easily see it as they completed the trip through the Bacalar Chico canal. At San Juan, we found pottery from the Yucatán, the south coast of Belize, as well as the Petén region of Guatemala and Campeche. We also found several vessels of Tohil Plumbate pottery which was made only on the Pacific Coast of Guatemala. There was gray obsidian from highland Guatemala and a surprising amount of green obsidian from Pachuca in central México. Green obsidian, like all green stone, was very much valued by the Maya and was traded by sea around the Yucatán. It was said that "...because its appearance is like a green Quetzal feather, it is precious, esteemed, valuable; it is worthy of being cherished; it merits storing; it is desirable, worthy of envy; it merits esteem and is praiseworthy."

In large ruins of northern Belize, about one percent of the obsidian is from Pachuca. At San Juan, well over 15 percent was from Pachuca. The people of San Juan also had access to some jade objects and basalt grinding tools from the Guatemalan highlands and had ground stone artifacts from Belize's

Maya Mountains.

Much of these materials were found in garbage deposits; others were found in burials. The Maya tended to bury people under their homes, or if they were rulers, perhaps in a tomb inside a temple. One burial from San Juan was of an infant child about three years old. The child was buried with a Late Classic cylinder vase and the pedestal base of a vessel dated several hundred years later. The cylinder vase had probably been a family heirloom. A male about 40 years old was interred with a Tohil Plumbate jar (the San Juan jar) and two other ceramic vessels, a carved jade face, a tubular jade bead, two stone knives and a stone flake, a carved shell bead, four deer antlers, and an awl made from a deer bone, and a manatee bone. This man was clearly important and may have been an expert stone worker; the deer antlers were exactly what would be used to fabricate stone tools.

One burial was not identified until we returned to our laboratories. We had excavated a burial with an offering inside two large dishes, one placed upside-down on the other so that they were resting lip to lip. Inside, we found what we first believed to be fish bones. It was only later that we found that this was the remains of a newborn or stillborn child. The reverence which the Maya showed for such a young life is indicative of their compassion.

Especially exciting among the artifacts at San Juan was the very high percentage of green obsidian recovered. Green obsidian comes only from the Pachuca area of central México and would need to be traded all the way around the Yucatán Peninsula to reach San Juan. Often, a few pieces of green obsidian are recovered in important tombs at main-

land sites. However, we found that almost 14 percent of the obsidian from San Juan was green Pachuca material. X-Ray Fluorescence of the gray obsidians also revealed that other pieces came from Michoacán and another still unknown Mexican source. Given San Juan's setting at the west side of the Bacalar Chico Canal, it is entirely possible that the green obsidian bound for northern Belize first stopped at San Juan.

The architecture of San Juan is also indicative of its role in the trade network. While no formal plaza exists at San Juan, buildings with mixed residential and administrative functions were found. Structure 3 is a building with a two-tiered round substructure and a small staircase leading to a round pole and thatch building on top. The entire arrangement sat on top of a rectangular platform. Round buildings like Structure 3 at San Juan are associated with influence and trade from northern Yucatán.

Another building, Structure 4, was very small and may have been used for storage. Its prominent location, adjacent to Structure 3, may indicate that it was used for the storage of valuable trade goods. Along one of its walls, we found a pile of notched potsherds. These are believed to have been used for weights on fishing nets and are still in use by contemporary fishermen. Perhaps someone had hung their net on the side of the building. Then the net fell to the ground, not to be disturbed again for a thousand years.

The latest date we have from San Juan is about 1,000 A.D., obtained from under a small house floor on the flanks of the main platform. It seems that after the main sector had been built, small

residences were constructed along the water's edge. These Terminal Classic people may have continued to use San Juan as a trade point, but we cannot be sure. Centuries later San Juan was visited by both Spanish and British sailors, as evidenced by the historic bottles and coins found there.

# Chac Balam

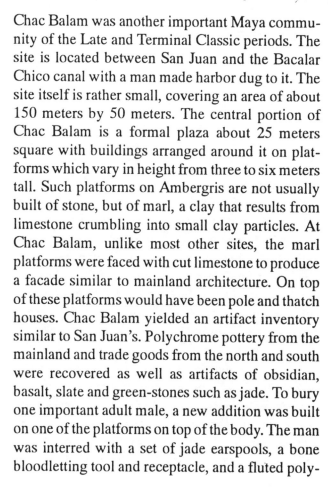

Chac Balam was another important Maya community of the Late and Terminal Classic periods. The site is located between San Juan and the Bacalar Chico canal with a man made harbor dug to it. The site itself is rather small, covering an area of about 150 meters by 50 meters. The central portion of Chac Balam is a formal plaza about 25 meters square with buildings arranged around it on platforms which vary in height from three to six meters tall. Such platforms on Ambergris are not usually built of stone, but of marl, a clay that results from limestone crumbling into small clay particles. At Chac Balam, unlike most other sites, the marl platforms were faced with cut limestone to produce a facade similar to mainland architecture. On top of these platforms would have been pole and thatch houses. Chac Balam yielded an artifact inventory similar to San Juan's. Polychrome pottery from the mainland and trade goods from the north and south were recovered as well as artifacts of obsidian, basalt, slate and green-stones such as jade. To bury one important adult male, a new addition was built on one of the platforms on top of the body. The man was interred with a set of jade earspools, a bone bloodletting tool and receptacle, and a fluted polychrome vessel probably made at Altun Ha. Underneath the burial was a cache that included a finely made black plate and two trickle-ware plates imported from the north. The bloodletting tool and blood receptacle were especially interesting as bloodletting was a ritual of the Maya elite. The evidence of such a ritual associated with this burial indicates that this man may have been the ruler of Chac Balam.

After the main occupation of Chac Balam, perhaps even after the site had been abandoned, a large number of very shallow burials were placed at the site. It is possible that Chac Balam was the ancestral home of people who at that time lived elsewhere and who returned to inter their dead.

Another kind of artifact found at Chac Balam and many other coastal sites, including Ek Luum, San Juan and Marco Gonzalez, is a pottery type named Coconut Walk Unslipped. Coconut Walk apparently was only made as very thin, shallow dishes about 40-50 cms in diameter. According to Elizabeth Graham and David Pendergast these were used for making salt by evaporating sea water. At Chac Balam, two plaster altars were excavated which were covered with Coconut Walk sherds. Also, Mound 1 at Ek Luum was a ritual location or temple of some sort. Enormous numbers of Coconut Walk sherds were also found there. With Coconut Walk found in such ritual contexts at Chac Balam and Ek Luum, we see reason to think that an alternative use for this pottery must exist. Finally, at least one lagoon on northern Ambergris, near San Juan and Chac Balam, produced salt well into this century. Since then, rising sea levels have made that lagoon no longer exploitable. It seems unlikely that, with a large local salt source nearby, the residents of these sites would devote much energy to making salt by evaporating sea water.

David Glassman has examined the skeletal remains of the burials from San Juan and Chac Balam. They appear to have had some of the problems shared by Mayas and other pre-industrial societies such as high infant mortality. However, they clearly were a very healthy population with very good nutrition and relatively little disease.

In general, the Late Classic sites on the west, or leeward, side of Ambergris Caye give us the impression of a successful and wealthy society. Trade goods from all over the Maya world were available to these people as were the easily accessible maritime resources for food. No doubt they had an enviable standard of living.

On the front side of the island, things were much different. Many small sites were found which do not have mounds. Where we excavated these sites, like the Franco site, we did not find plazas and large platforms for buildings. Instead there were only the buried, thin plaster floors left from small perishable houses. Only a very few people could have lived at each of these sites, perhaps a family or two. The pottery was very crudely made and no imported artifacts were found. While people in the wealthier sites used obsidian and high quality stone tools imported from the mainland, the people

at the small windward side sites often made tools of shell. These people probably made a living by fishing. Although they had few 'expensive' possessions, their lives were probably quite comfortable. It appears that the wealth of the sea was more than enough to satisfy their needs.

Other larger communities dating to the Late Classic period are also found on the windward side of Ambergris Caye. Typically, these sites cover several hundred square meters and some of them, such as Mata Grande, Tres Cocos and Habaneros, benefited from long distance trade. While we have not excavated at these sites, surface collections yielded sherds of high quality, imported pottery and artifacts such as basalt grinding stones and obsidian blades from remote areas. Generally these sites do not have monumental architecture, such as structures built on top of platforms as temples. Nevertheless, the inhabitants seem to have thrived in a mixed fishing and trading economy.

# Ek Luum

Ek Luum is one of the largest of these sites. Located about 250 meters from the present beach, Ek Luum is typical of the windward sites in that it is far enough away from the beach for safety, yet close enough for easy access. It was also built on the shore of the Laguna Cantena within sight of communities like Burning Water and Chac Balam. The major portion of the site is a raised area about 140 meters by 120 meters, elevated about 2.5 meters above the surrounding terrain. Excavations have demonstrated that this area grew gradually by the construction of houses upon the remains of older houses for several hundred years. This is unlike Chac Balam and San Juan where relatively large scale construction projects created the sites as we see them today. Unlike other windward side sites, Ek Luum includes monumental architecture as well as residences. Mound 1 is an earthen mound approximately four meters in height over-looking the Laguna Cantena which was capped by a series of marl floors. Thousands of sherds of Coconut Walk pottery were recovered from this structure. These probably are the result of ritual activity at Mound 1. Mound 2 is also about four meters above the surrounding area, but unlike Mound 1, residential debris was found there. Per-haps Mound 2 was the residence of the priest and Mound 1 was the location of public ceremonies.

While some exotic goods were found at Ek Luum, it was with much less frequency than at San Juan and Chac Balam. Several obsidian blades were found inside a small building much like Structure 4 at San Juan, which may have also been a storage building. Also, a cache of two pottery vessels was found. In general, though, the people of Ek Luum did not have access to the large quantities of exotic materials that their neighbors did. They used less elaborate pottery and more commonly used shell tools instead of tools of the high quality stone which came to the island from the 'chert-bearing zone' of northern Belize near Orange Walk Town.

The Late Classic period seems to have been a time of much population expansion on Ambergris, as it was elsewhere. Numerous small sites on the island's lagoons were occupied. On the north side of San Pedro Lagoon, at least seven small occupa-tional areas have been identified. Probably, many

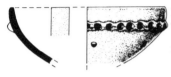

more exist, but intense and detailed surveys would be required to have any idea of just how many such sites do exist on the island.

Finding that the Maya had been heavily involved in maritime trade during the Classic period really was not a great surprise. We knew that such trade was extremely important during the Postclassic, so its roots would surely have to be found in the Classic period. The great surprise was that the coastal margins of Ambergris were largely abandoned by 1000 A.D.. There were exceptions, however. The community of Marco Gonzalez continued to thrive and new buildings were being constructed while other sites on the island were being abandoned. The tiny site of Los Renegados also had an interesting Postclassic occupation. Tantalizing clues about the nature of the Ambergris Caye Maya during the Postclassic may also be found at the site of Basil Jones.

# Marco Gonzalez

The Marco Gonzalez site may be the largest ruin on Ambergris Caye. Located about two miles south of the town of San Pedro, it covers an area of about 355 meters by 155 meters and has at least 53 buildings with a central plaza and several small courtyard groupings. The site's excavators believe that during the Early Classic period, the economy of Marco Gonzalez was based upon exploitation of the vast marine resources which the Caribbean provides. The community saw continued success through the Late Classic period as well. However, during the Postclassic period, when other sites on Ambergris were being abandoned, Marco Gonzalez underwent large scale expansion. Nearly every one of the structures were added to or used at this time.

Even more importantly, it was at this time that Marco Gonzalez became a trade outpost for the great mainland center of Lamanai. Lamanai, the second largest site in Belize, survived and thrived through the 'Maya collapse'. It may well have done so because of its strategic location on the New River Lagoon. While other great centers, such as La Milpa and Río Azul, were abandoned, Lamanai had the opportunity to become a funnel for forest and agricultural goods of the eastern Petén and northern Belize regions to enter the maritime trade system. Goods were shipped from Lamanai to Marco Gonzalez where they were trans-shipped onto coastal canoes in exchange for other commodities and exotic goods. Both Lamanai and Marco Gonzalez flourished into the 13th century, well after the end of the Maya civilization in much of the rest of Belize. It is even possible that the community of Marco Gonzalez persisted until the mid-15th century.

Like the sites of Chac Balam and San Juan, Marco Gonzalez has yielded an interesting array of exotic artifacts. These include green and gray obsidian as well as pottery from Yucatán and elsewhere. One burial included a Tohil Plumbate pot which was virtually identical to one excavated at San Juan. The similarity is so close that we suspect that they were made by the same potter. What makes this so remarkable is that Plumbate pottery was made only in one small region of Guatemala's northwest Pacific coast. It is usually found in very small quantities as burial offerings or in other ritually significant contexts. The four Plumbate vessels known to have been found on Ambergris Caye are actually a surprisingly large number.

Another site, Los Renegados physically resembles the small marine oriented sites like the Franco site. However, looks are often deceiving. Los Renegados has no mounds and appears to be only a black dirt deposit. The precise size of the site is not known, probably only a few hundred square meters. The only evidence of houses at the site are the very thin, buried plaster floors found in test excavations. However, Los Renegados yielded a collection of nearly 200 obsidian blades, all from sources in the Guatemalan highlands. Almost all of the pottery from the site is of the Paxcaman series, possibly from the Tulum region. This surprising site indicates that Postclassic activity was certainly occurring on the island, but we have no way of knowing much about the nature of that activity.

# Basil Jones

The other site on Ambergris Caye which probably dates to the Postclassic period is Basil Jones. South of Rocky Point at the interior of the island is Ambergris Caye's widest section. It is much higher and supports a much different vegetation pattern. Here there is a series of crudely built stone mounds, now nearly destroyed by looting and, perhaps, by the work of Ambergris's first archaeologist, Thomas Gann. This British physician, explorer and archaeologist is famous for probing into nearly every site in northern Belize. It was he who discovered the important murals at Santa Rita and first excavated at Lubaantun. En route to Belize City by boat in the 1920s, Gann made a stop on Ambergris to excavate the 'largest mound' on the northern part of the island. He wrote that:

"several burial mounds were excavated, in which bones were disturbed, the skeletons lying on their backs... and food offerings in pottery receptacles provided for their journey into the next world, indicating the usual method of burial among these people. A second mound was excavated, which had been built over the ruins of a small stone chamber. Nothing was found within it, but beneath the centre was discovered a round saucer for burning incense, with a long handle, and a curious figurine in clay, whose face was covered by a peculiar grilled arrangement, more resembling a baseball mask than anything else, which was studded with rossettes." (Gann, 1926: 60).

The ceramic incensario which Gann describes is clearly from the Postclassic period and the mounds are probably those of Basil Jones.

An important feature of Basil Jones is the network of stone walls which apparently surrounded privately owned fields. Such wall systems have also been found on Cozumel Island and several other locations along the coast of the state of Quintana Roo, México, north of Ambergris. Unlike much of the rest of the island, the higher northern interior has reasonably fertile land which could have been used for farming. If, as we believe, these fields are Postclassic, then Basil

Jones represents a major shift in the island economy, away from trading and fishing to an agricultural base.

This shift may have been forced upon the residents of Ambergris Caye to some degree. The late Eric Thompson put forth the idea that a Maya group, the Putún from the Tabasco coast, began to seize control of Maya trade routes at the end of the Classic period. They may well have taken over existing trade routes and consolidated them into one great network. It is also true that Postclassic ports such as Tulum and Ixpaatún were spread further apart than the Classic ports before them. The later ports were also larger and defended from land attacks. This is just what might occur if a large and powerful group forced local 'Mom-and-Pop' operations out of business. Then, the Putún would have needed to carefully locate and defend their outposts from pirates and raiders from competing groups. A French-Mexican expedition led by Michel Piessel in 1988 was able to show that coastal traders could easily travel 30 or more miles in a single day. Certainly, it was not necessary to have ports located every four or five miles as they were on Ambergris in the Classic period.

Whatever the cause, Ambergris Caye in the Postclassic period no longer seems to have had the important role in maritime trade which it enjoyed in the Classic period. The shift to a farming economy at Basil Jones on the interior of the island at the same time coastal margin sites, such as Chac Balam and San Juan, are abandoned may have occurred because of this 'horizontal integration' of the coastal trade system by the Putún Maya. It has been thought that the Maya had abandoned Ambergris Caye long before Europeans arrived.

However, a tantalizing clue to the contrary, a map recently located in the Spanish archives at Seville appears to indicate a settlement on northern Ambergris Caye in the general area of Basil Jones. Other similar notations on the same map are of colonial missions. Of course, where there are missions, there must be Maya for the friars to missionize. Perhaps then, Basil Jones holds the key to understanding the last chapter of the Maya on Ambergris Caye before modern times.

A thousand years ago, the maritime traders of Ambergris had built a large and affluent society. Today, San Pedro and Ambergris Caye are growing again. We do not know how many people lived on the island in the past, but certainly it was more than today. Though it is difficult to know how these people lived, it is clear that the resources of the sea and the wealth from maritime commerce allowed them to live very well indeed.

# Other Publications

Glassman, David, and James F. Garber
  1999 Land Use, Diet, and Their Effects on
       the Biology of the Prehistoric Maya
       of Northern Ambergris Cay, Belize. In
       *Reconstructing Ancient Maya Diet,*
       edited by Christine White. University
       of Utah Press, Provo.

Graham, Elizabeth, and David Pendergast
  1989 Excavations at the Marco Gonzalez
       Site, Ambergris Caye, Belize. *Journal
       of Field Archaeology* 16:1–16.

Guderjan, Thomas H.
  1988 Maya Trade at San Juan, Ambergris
       Caye, Belize. Ph.D. dissertation, De-
       partment of Anthropology, Southern
       Methodist University, Dallas.
  1995 Maya Settlement and Trade on Amber-
       gris Caye, Belize. *Ancient Mesoamerica*
       6:147–159.
  2004 Elite Burial Rites from the Site of Chac
       Balam on Ambergris Caye, Belize.
       *Mexicon* 26(4):98–102

Guderjan, Thomas H., and James F. Garber
  1995 *Maya Maritime Trade, Settlement, and
       Populations on Ambergris Caye, Belize.*
       Labyrinthos, Culver City, California.

Guderjan, Thomas H., James F. Garber, Herman Smith, Fred Stross, Helen Michel, and Frank Asaro

1989 Maya Maritime Trade and Sources of Obsidian at San Juan, Ambergris Cay, Belize. *Journal of Field Archaeology* 16(4):363–369.

Guderjan, Thomas H., and Lorraine A. Williams-Beck

2001 Another Dimension of Trade and Inter-action on Ambergris Caye, Belize. *Mexicon* 18(5):123–125.

Stemp, James

2001 Chipped Stone Tool Use in the Maya Coastal Economies of Marco Gonzalez and San Pedro, Ambergris Caye, Belize. BAR International Series 935. Oxford, England.